# Puss in Boots

George Ivanoff
Illustrated by Diane Le Feyer

Once upon a time,
there was a story about a cat.
The cat wore boots.

Sarah and Joe went to the library
to read the story.
As they started to read...

...a fairy appeared!
"I am Fifi the Fairytale Fixit Fairy," she said.
"This story is broken.
Can you help me fix it?"

Fifi waved her wand.

Sarah and Joe fell into the book.

They landed on a path.

A cat was sitting by the side of the path.
There was a pair of boots next to him.

The cat was licking his paws.

"What's the matter?" asked Sarah.
"The boots," said the cat.
"They hurt my feet."

"You have to wear the boots," said Sarah. "The story is called 'Puss in Boots'!"

The cat shook his head.
“What can we do?” asked Joe.

"I know!" Sarah smiled. "Socks!"
Sarah took off her shoes and socks.

Sarah gave her socks to the cat.

Joe gave his socks to the cat, too.
"Sorry," said Joe.
"They are a bit stinky!"

The cat put on the socks and the boots.
“My feet don’t hurt any more!” he said.

"Thank you for fixing the story," said Fifi.
"Now, let's go shopping."
"Why?" asked Sarah and Joe.
"We need to get you new socks!" said Fifi.